What is Suicide?

A Book to Explain
a Loss From Suicide
to Children

written by **McKenzie Blumhagen**

illustrated by **Annie Larson**

What is Suicide?
A Book to Explain A Loss From Suicide to Children

© 2023, McKenzie Blumhagen.

ISBN: 979-8-35093-124-2

A letter from the author to the adult reader of this book:

Can I just give you a tear jerking, safe, tight, hug through these pages? The journey of deep grief you are navigating is one of the most challenging forms of grief I have ever experienced myself. You are left with questions, replaying circumstances, and wondering if there was anything that could have been done. It is a painful circle of mental and emotional torture. Losing our loved ones to a form of darkness is never simple. I have been to more funerals than I am years old, and the ones for suicide have always been more dynamically challenging for me. Losses from non-natural causes can just have a different, not less impactful, but different influence on those of us left here on earth.

As a woman of faith, I encourage you to pour your questions you have about grief to God. These losses are not intended to carry alone and there are times where you feel like others on earth just cannot understand the pain, but God can, and He does. I surely do not have the answers, but I have turned to God with every loss of suicide I have experienced, and it is the reason I am writing this letter to you.

My prayer and encouragement to you is this: Pray and pray fiercely for your heart to be protected by His peace and truth. Pray for wisdom on how to navigate the grief alongside your friends and family. Pray for how to have conversations about this loss. Pray & trust that we serve an all-merciful God who understands every depth of evil on this earth. The God Questions, especially in darkness, can bring us closer to Him if we are willing to keep our hearts and ears open to his comfort and guidance.

About the Author:

McKenzie Kay Blumhagen was raised in North Dakota by her mother—Shauna Schneider, stepfather—Mark Schneider, and father—Greg Darling. She comes from an agricultural background with her mom and stepdad having a multigenerational farming operation, but she never imagined marrying a farmer. Little did she know, she fell in love with one just like that. Her husband—Ryan Blumhagen, and herself have a farmstead in rural North Dakota where they are raising their two daughters, - Isabelle & Eloise alongside their trusted Golden Retriever, Sedona.

The advocacy for Suicide Prevention is embedded into McKenzie after the loss of her cousin R.J., who you will see is one of the main characters of this book. It was only a year after his loss that McKenzie was treated as an in-patient in a psychiatric facility for her own suicidal ideation and self-harming behaviors. McKenzie has traveled to high schools around North Dakota to share her story and to educate students about how to cope with the overwhelming emotions they are encountering in their stage of life. Her hope and prayer are the conversations do not stop there.

Her most profound memory of sharing her story with students was a time when she was on her way to a high school, and she rolled her car on black ice. She landed upside down. She was safely able to release herself from her seatbelt and by some miracle, the state snow removal plow was going by and stopped to helped her exit her vehicle. She was able to call everybody necessary. She truly felt like something was trying to hold her back from reaching those students that day. With limited service she successfully reached her mother and asked her to call the school she was heading to and inform them she would be late.

Her mother gasped at the idea but did as she was asked. McKenzie was injury free with not even a scratch, Praise God! McKenzie's stepfather came to drive her the rest of the way and she spoke to all three audiences that afternoon. Her husband calls it her "Teddy Roosevelt moment in time."

*My prayer is that this book helps you navigate
the challenging conversation about a loss from suicide.*

The first verse I ever memorized after I was hospitalized was Jeremiah 29:11

**"For I know the plans I have for you, declares the Lord,
Plans for welfare and not for evil, to give you a future and a hope."**

I truly believe we serve a Merciful God. The children he has lost to suicide breaks I lis heart as much as it is impacting your life. That pain is eternal for Him, so you are not alone in your grief. God has helped heal me through my own hospitalization as well as through healing from the grief of multiple losses of suicide. However, in those valleys of suffering, when I find myself swallowed in fears, I lean into this verse,

Psalm 101:13-14 states

*"As a father shows compassion to his children, so the Lord shows compassion to those
who fear him. For He knows how we are formed; he remembers that we are dust."*

He loves every child He created. Lean into that. He loves all of you reading this book, and He loves the person you lost that lead you to find this story. He is grieving with you.

About the Illustrator:

Annie Larson is a mother and wife to a beautiful family in rural Minnesota. Annie & McKenzie met and became fast friends when McKenzie & Ryan pursued and purchased a home Annie & Travis listed for sale. Annie also comes from an agricultural background and is raising her family similarly to how she grew up.

Her outward creativity and ever-changing paths of expression are what define Annie as a true artist. Annie lets no dust settle under her feet. She juggles her passions of being a chocolatier, to pursuing and tackling her own house building projects, to creating art in sketches and paintings. She truly embraces a beautiful gift from God that speaks through her creations, and she strengthens that gift by using it consistently.

When I was pursuing an illustrator for this book, I knew it had to be someone I trusted with the delicacy of the content and the characters. Annie accepted the offer immediately and it was the first-person I had shared the written story with. Annie responded with absolute encouragement and dove into the illustrations using childhood photos of myself & RJ shared from my family. You can appreciate more of her talent in her art below.

This book is written in memory of
Dan Darling, R.J. Darling, Tony Rayer, Jesse Economy, and Andy Berg.

These are the lives of my personal family members
and dear friend that were all lost to suicide.

It is their losses that taught me about the grief that comes from suicide.

I remember the delivery of the news for all of these losses and from the first one being when I was very young to the last one being in the process of publishing this book, the pain of a loss from suicide rears an ugly face. It is from my prayer time after these losses that has motivated me to finally put these pages into the world.

Unfortunately, the impact of loss from suicide is getting younger and the conversations are getting much more challenging to navigate. So, as much as I hoped this book was not one a family would "need" to read, I also wanted to create a resource for the many families that desired something to better help them explain this type of loss to children.

**This book is written with permission from the family of R.J. Darling.
You will notice R.J. & McKenzie are the main characters in this children's story.**

McKenzie was just a kid, but she was quite intuitive just like you are. She was hanging out in her bedroom by her desk, and she remembered her teacher teaching her all about feelings. She was remembering her teacher saying, "Intuitive means that you know that someone is sad when you see them crying, or that you know they are mad when you see their face is red or their arms are crossed or if they are stomping away." McKenzie was imagining sitting on the carpet with her friends and her teacher telling her all of this again.

She remembers her teacher leaning in close to her and her friends and saying, "Now when you are friends with someone who is sad, you feel sad for them, or when people are acting silly, you join them and begin acting silly too. That is what friends do even if they are adults!"

McKenzie came out of her room and realized some family had come over. She was sensing that the people around her were very sad as she heard them talking downstairs. She listened closer and she heard them say, "It's so sad, he was so young to die from suicide."

McKenzie knew what it meant to die, but she did not know what suicide was.

When McKenzie's mother walked upstairs, McKenzie went into the hallway. Her mom seemed sad, so McKenzie asked her mom, "Mom, do you need a hug?" McKenzie's mom said, "I would love one."

McKenzie was confused about who died and what the word suicide meant so she asked her mom, "Mom, what is suicide?" Her mother looked surprised and replied with a sigh, "Oh McKenzie, did you hear us talking about R.J.?" McKenzie nodded yes. "Well sweetheart, suicide is when somebody dies because their brain was sick, and it made their heart really sad all of the time. Do you know what it feels like to be sad?" McKenzie said, "Yes, I know what it feels like to be sad. It is when people cry because they are hurt, or someone said something mean to them."

McKenzie's mom had a soft smile letting McKenzie know that she understood what it felt like to be sad, but then she told McKenzie, "Yes sweetheart, that is what it feels like to be sad for some people. Other people, when they are sad, they try to hide it. Have you ever seen someone try to hide being sad?" McKenzie nodded yes and said, "Yeah mom, sometimes when friends are sad in school, they put their head down at the table so that nobody can see them crying."

Her mom nodded, "Yes just like that but sometimes when big kids or adults hide it, they don't put their head down. They cry in places people cannot see or they try really really hard not to cry and then they can act very angry. Do you know what it means to feel angry?"

McKenzie looked at her mother and replied "Yes, being angry is when your entire body feels super-duper tight. Sometimes people yell, or say mean things, or even throw things. I have been angry before, Mom." McKenzie's mother said, "It is okay to feel angry sometimes, everybody can feel angry sometimes. There are people who are really sad and don't want other people to see it. When they hide it for too long, their sadness can turn into anger, and when they get angry, their brain makes them yell, or say mean things, or even throw things. They might even hurt themselves or other people. And then, when they are already mad, their brain starts telling them things that make them feel even more sad and angry."

McKenzie looked at her mom with a confused look on her face. Her mom continued, "Their brains can tell them words like, "You aren't good at doing anything, or that that nobody likes them. It says really hurtful mean things to them that can make things worse. Do you understand?" McKenzie started to feel really sad and told her mom, "Those are really mean things mom. I would feel really sad if my brain said those things to me."

15

McKenzie's mom started crying as she said, "I would too. And R.J. was very sad too. His brain said so many mean things that he hurt himself and now we won't get to see him alive again." McKenzie looked at her dresser where she had a picture of her and R.J. celebrating one of their birthdays together and she got really sad. And then she asked her mom, "Do other people get so sad that they hurt themselves too?" McKenzie's mom cried and said "Yes, other people feel the same way R.J. did and they hurt themselves too."

McKenzie told her mom "We need to teach people that we are not supposed to hurt ourselves when we are hurt and that it is dangerous. We need my teacher to teach everyone about feelings; she is really good at it."

McKenzie's mom hugged her a little tighter, and she cried a little more. McKenzie started to cry too.

They waited in McKenzie's room until they both wanted to go downstairs to see the rest of the family that had come to the house.

The next pages are going to cover feeling words to explore that promote emotional health for children. We know the stigma is alive when it comes to talking about mental health. Raising the next generation to use the correct vocabulary for their feelings and the conversations around them will normalize healthy discussions around emotional wellbeing.

My prayer is that as we immerse children with regulation strategies, the stigma will dissipate, and we will have a more sustained emotional health as a society.

These definitions may be modified to use child-friendly language. The original definitions can be found using the Britannica dictionary online. See the sources page:

<u>WORRY:</u>

to think about problems or things we are afraid (scared) of.

Use this extra space to draw a face of someone who might be **worried:**

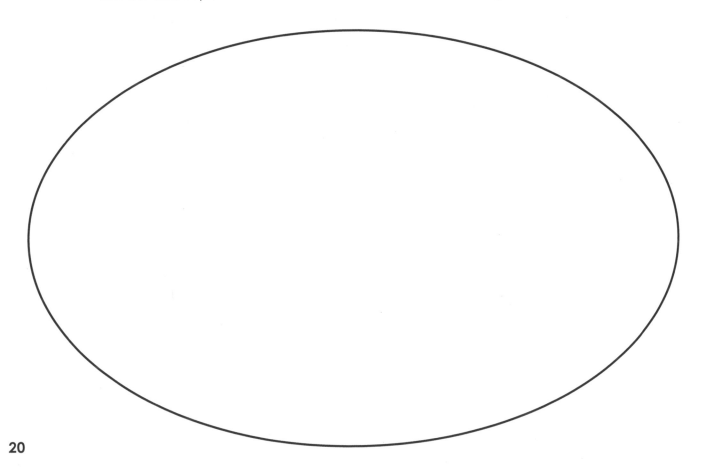

<u>HAPPY:</u>

feeling of joy. This feeling makes us smile and feel good inside.

Use this extra space to draw a face of someone who might be **happy:**

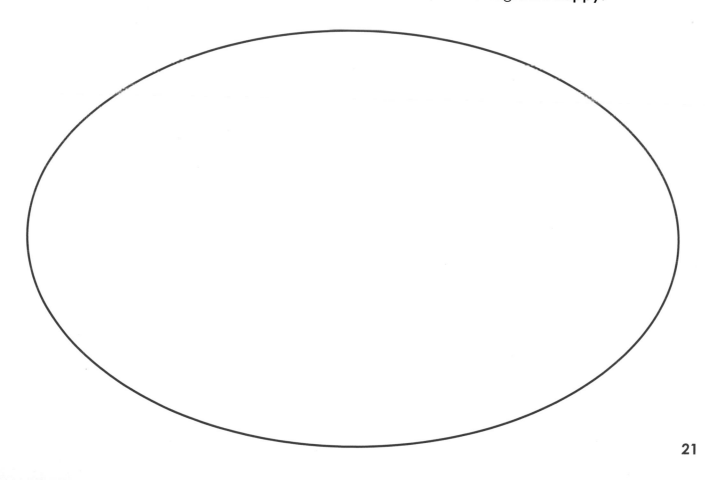

21

<u>SAD:</u>

not feeling happy. This feeling might make us cry.

We might feel this way when we get hurt.

Use this extra space to draw a face of someone who might be **sad:**

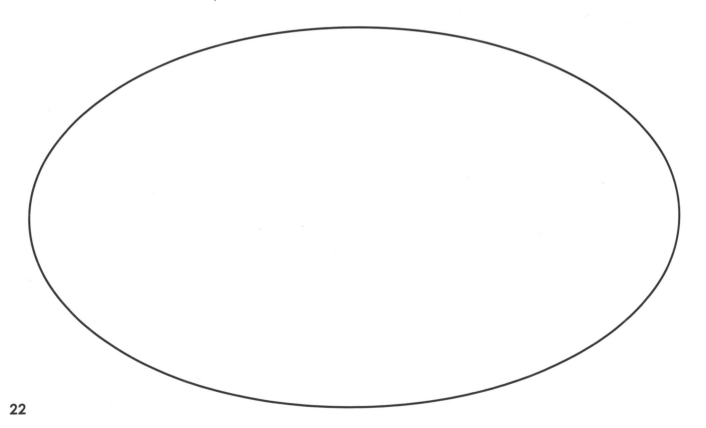

ANXIOUS:

afraid (scared) or nervous

especially about what may happen.

Use this extra space to draw a face of someone who might be **anxious:**

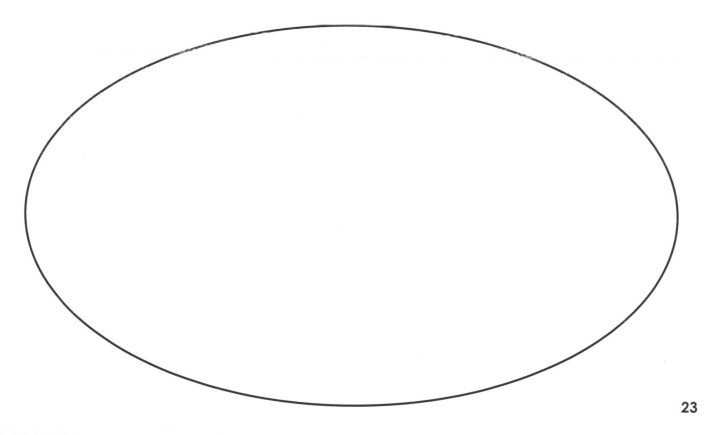

ANGER:

a strong feeling of being upset or annoyed because of something wrong or bad: the feeling that makes someone want to hurt other people, to shout.

Use this extra space to draw a face of someone who might be **angry:**

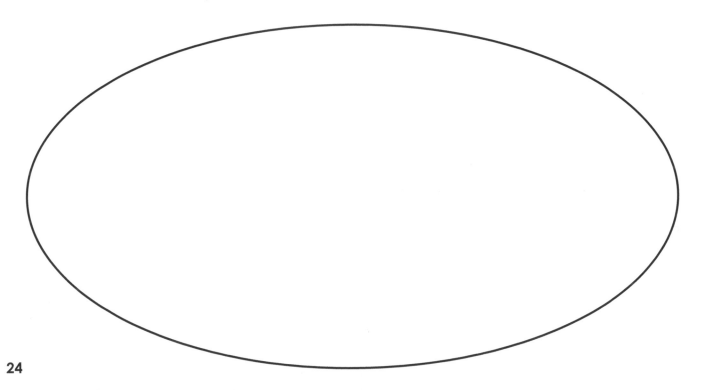

<u>SAFE:</u>

not able or likely to be hurt or harmed in any way:

not in danger

Use this extra space to draw a face of someone who might be **safe:**

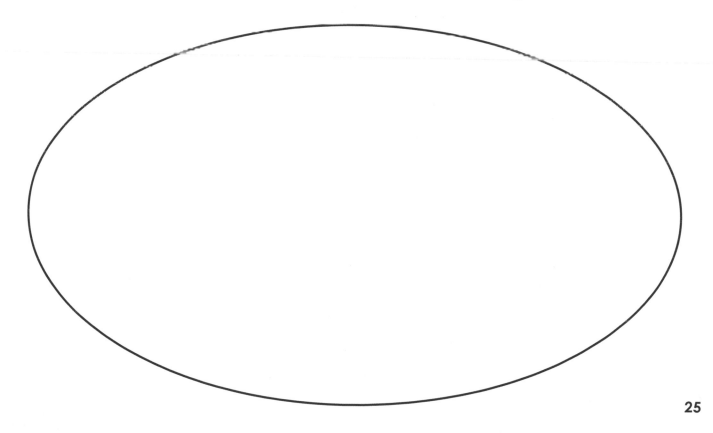

SAFE SPACE:

a place you go when you need to calm down. We all like different things and places. This place is for YOU. There might be pillows, coloring books, colored pencils, or Legos. You think of a space where you would feel safe and could calm down if you were feeling angry or a space that would help you cheer up if you were sad.

Draw & color that place below.

Sources:

Encyclopædia Britannica, Encyclopædia Britannica, inc., www.britannica.com/dictionary.
Accessed 26 Aug. 2023.